Rycote Chapel

OXFORDSHIRE

JOHN SALMON BA, FSA

Rycote Chapel is one of those attractive places of worship, sometimes a private chapel, sometimes parochial, but always appearing to be connected first and foremost with a great house. One thinks of Staunton Harold in Leicestershire, Langley in Shropshire, Steane in Northamptonshire, Gibside in County Durham, or Gwydir and Rûg in North Wales. They are generally buildings which have escaped insensitive Victorian restoration. They often lie at the end of an overgrown drive and survive in their entirety while the great house may well have disappeared altogether or have degenerated into a farmhouse or become an institution. Rycote lies at the end of a short drive turning off the Thame-Wallingford road.

The great house shown in the views by Winstanley (c.1695) and Kip (1714) was burnt out in 1745 and finally pulled down in 1800, though there is still a building of mellowed Tudor brick on a stone base with a stepped gable which is marked as 'The Stables' on Winstanley's view and was carefully restored soon after 1911 to form a pleasant home of moderate size, a function that, happily, it still performs.

ENGLISH HERITAGE · LONDON

CONTENTS

WORLD
LAND
TRUST™

www.carbonbalancedpaper.com
CBP00022661101131814

Published by English Heritage
1 Waterhouse Square, 138-142 Holborn, London EC1N 2ST
© Crown copyright 1967
Previously published by HMSO 1980
First published by English Heritage 1988, reprinted 1996, 2007, 2010, 2013
Printed in England by Pureprint
Dd 6073922, 01/13, C10, 0563, 38776, FA5819
ISBN 978-1-85074-215-9

DESCRIPTION

Rycote Chapel from the south-east

Exterior of the chapel

The chapel was consecrated in 1449. Stone from the Taynton quarries near Burford had been used for its building. The dressed stonework is still in good condition; the middle retains a little of its protective plaster on its east and north sides. It was a chantry foundation with three priests attached to it. Of the other buildings nothing remains. The chapel is without aisles and there is no structural division between nave and chancel other than a rise of one step internally, which may not be original. (Refer to the plan.)

The tower is divided into three stages by string courses. In its western face the lowest stage has an acutely pointed west doorway and above it a three-light window with shields of Quatremayne and Englefield terminating the dripstone. The north and south walls at this stage are blank. The second stage has on its western face a very attractive tall canopied niche with an octagonal pedestal for a statue. At the back of the niche is a small light which can have been of little practical use if a statue were ever placed here, other than devotional. On the north and south faces are rectangular-headed single-light windows surmounted by a dripstone as are all the tower windows. The third stage has belfry windows on all four sides, a single light on the south side, and a two light on the other three sides.

The staircase turret is contained in the south-east angle. It projects slightly on the south side but not on the east, and it is not heightened above the level of the battlements. It is lighted by five small windows all of different form, starting from the bottom: (1) a trefoil, (2) rectangular, (3) a quatrefoil, (4) simple pointed head, (5) pointed with trefoil head. All face south-west. Stepped buttresses at the north-east, north-west and south-west corners reach nearly to the top of the second stage of the tower. The latter two are set diagonally to the walls, while that at the north-east corner lies against the north wall, its lowest stage being flush with the north wall of the nave. The tower is a simple, pleasing and well-proportioned structure, especially when viewed across the greensward to the west of the chapel.

The body of the chapel is about 8ft (2.4m) wider than the tower. The north and south walls are divided into five sections by buttresses, five on each side. The buttresses have a debased form of crocketed finial, except the two at the east end which are surmounted by chained beasts (much renewed), the middle buttress on the south side which has a spiral finial, the south-west finial which is rebuilt and plain, and the north-west which is a chimney, the use of which will be discussed later. The middle buttress on the north side is of greater width to contain the rood loft staircase.

Between the first and second buttresses from the west on the north side is a Tudor-arched doorway which faces the site of the house and was presumably the entrance used by its occupants. The doorway is set in a rectangular frame, the horizontal member of which is adorned with three shields (the middle one at an angle), now blank but probably originally painted. The spandrels of the arch are filled with

quatrefoils. The dripstone is supported on the east by a human head with flat cap and flowing hair and on the west by a more weather-worn and grotesque head which dies into the adjacent buttress. The doorway in the corresponding position on the south side, which is now the entrance, is quite plain and was obviously of less importance.

The priest's small doorway is in the north wall of the chancel, which suggests the chantry house was on this side. It has a more acutely pointed arch and the fragments of two plain shields at the end of the dripstone. There are five windows on both north and south sides, each with two cinquefoiled lights and with dripstones, again terminating in blank shields. A large window fills most of the east wall. It consists of five lights, each light subdivided into two in the head of the window. Above is a small plain triangular window lighting the area between the ceiling and the roof. Built here and there into the walls are thin tiles.

The roof is tiled and at the east end are the base and lower part of the stem of a gable cross. To the south of the chapel are a large yew tree (said to have been planted to mark the coronation of King Stephen in 1135) and a few gravestones including two, presumably a 'header' and a 'footer,' to Jane Flambert who died on 21 April 1731.

Interior of the chapel

From the outside the chapel appears to be a mid-fifteenth-century building with nothing in particular to make it stand out from many other churches in the district. It is only on entering and catching a first glimpse of the interior that one realises that the seventeenth-century fittings make this a chapel of outstanding interest. This work belongs to two periods: the earlier *c*.1610 which covers the western gallery, the two large pews and the pulpit; the

later *c.*1682, the date of the present reredos. To a third and earlier period, *c.*1449, the date of the original foundation, belong the simpler wooden seating in the nave and the chancel, the base and cover of the font and the base of the rood screen.

Just within the west door on the south wall slight traces were once visible of what might have been a painted black border containing black-letter texts from the seventeenth century. Traces of wall paintings have been found elsewhere, for instance on the east wall behind the reredos.

Beneath the west gallery is the font, a plain circular bowl from the twelfth century. This suggests that there may have been an earlier domestic chapel on the site. Some carved stonework of thirteenth-century date showing dog-tooth ornament and a stiff-leafed foliage capital, now preserved at the present house, are said to have been dug up at Rycote at some date prior to 1928. The font suggests the chapel had the right of baptism, a prerogative often retained by the parish church, in this case Great Haseley. The lower quarter of the font bowl was recut to give it an octagonal form so as to fit better on to the fifteenth-century octagonal base, each side of which has a trefoil-headed arch showing traces of colouring. The recut lower section of the bowl was also painted, possibly in the seventeenth century, with shields the charges of which are now almost inde-cipherable. The fifteenth-century canopied font cover is octagonal and quite plain apart from the moulded ribs and the finial. A hook on the latter suggests some simple form of pulley to raise and lower the cover.

The western gallery is supported to the east by tapering, circular columns (two in the middle and a half column at each end) with Ionic capitals rather similar to those on the 1610 reredos, now hung under the tower. The ringed bases of the columns stand on square bases about 2ft 6in (75cm) tall, the two in the middle being decorated

with a form of split baluster. The gallery front is balustraded and divided into three sections. The ceiling beneath the tower and gallery is painted as one whole in red and blue representing cloud and stars.

The nave is floored with plain red tiles into which are let four lozenge-shaped memorial stones commemorating (1) Elizabeth Goddard, gentlewoman to Eleonora, Countess of Abingdon, died 1696; (2) John Connop, 'Several years Ranger of Rycot Park,' died 1707 and Norreys Connop his son 'who succeeded him,' died 1727; (3) Margaret Tilly, wife of William Tilly, DD, Rector of Albury, died 1717; (4) Sir John Collins, died 1763. In a fulsome description typical of the period Margaret Tilly is described as 'a person exemplary for ye truest ornament of her sex an humble, meek, and quiet spirit, of a conversation innocent, inoffensive, justly chearful, delightful, and useful, of a life strictly vertuous, sincerely pious, prudent, patient and charitable, delighting and desirous to do good to all.' On the south wall is a simple memorial tablet inscribed 'In memory of Alfred St George Hamersley KC, JP, MP 1910-18 who lived at Rycote 1911-29 and preserved this chapel.' It is fitting that one who did so much to maintain the chapel in the early years of the present century should be so commemorated.

Almost all the original fifteenth-century seating remains in the nave. It consists of backed benches with simple rectangular ends, small buttresses being their only decoration. Against the north wall within the third pew is a fireplace. The grate is obviously later and the whole thing may be an insertion. However, there is no evidence for an enclosed pew here and the flue and chimney are contained in the westernmost of the buttresses on the north side which otherwise appears to be fifteenth-century. Speculation as to its date and purpose includes the suggestion that it

could perhaps have been an oven for baking wafers for the mass, a rare feature and always found in the chancel, as, for example, at Dedham Church in Essex.

Further east on the south side is the early seventeenth-century pulpit, typical work of the period though it is square rather than octagonal as was the more usual fashion. Each of the three detached sides is decorated with four rectangular panels, in pairs above each other. Apart from one panel facing east the upper pairs are carved with a semicircular arch resting on crude Ionic capitals and spirally decorated columns. Scrollwork separates the panels. The lower panels are carved with a lozenge design.

This decoration is repeated on the backboard of the pulpit. Its flat rectangular tester (sounding board) is attached to the wall by an iron rod and it has a dado on each side of two very flattened arches decorated with a fretted pattern in relief. The underside of the tester is also carved and divided into four panels. Below is the reader's pew.

The fifteenth-century wagon roof is continuous over the nave and chancel. It is ceiled with horizontal boards on which survives much evidence of a later painted decorative scheme associated with the seventeenth-century work elsewhere in the church. Considerable traces of red are still visible on the woodwork. In addition scores of golden stars were attached to the laths, each about 2in (50mm) across and cut out of cardboard, possibly in some cases from playing cards as the back of a few show a heart or diamond. A small area of the ceiling at the west end has been reconstructed showing gold stars on a blue background. When the whole scene was complete the general effect must have been very colourful, recalling on a more modest scale such painted ceilings as at Bromfield Priory in Shropshire (1672) or at Gwydir Chapel in North Wales (1673).

The lower part of the medieval rood screen survives as the eastern wall of both the large pews. In the early seventeenth century an open arcading, of classical columns about 3ft (1m) high surmounted by semicircular arches and with a formalised foliage design in the spandrels on the east side, was erected on top of this, with a wide semicircular arch forming the entrance into the chancel between the pews. This arch is surmounted by an elaborate strapwork design similar to that which in a like position formerly enclosed the Royal Arms at St John's Church in Leeds (1634).

The open arcading continues round the south and west sides of the northern pew. On the north side is a plain fifteenth-century door, of three vertical planks, opening on to the former rood loft stairs, later adapted to give access to the loft above the pew. The north wall east of the door is filled with panelling divided into four rows, each of three panels. All of these contain an oval within which was painted a picture; little is now visible though three retain traces of a townscape and one of a human figure. On the base of the rood screen facing into the pew the original cinquefoiled carved heads of each panel remain, but in three of the four bays the dividing mullions have been broken away to form larger areas of surface which were painted with an elaborate starlike pattern. This design is also carried round the south and west sides of the pew.

The seating against the walls of the pew is quite plain. The ceiling is painted with stars and blue clouds, rather similar to that beneath the west gallery. Two simple circular columns help to support the south side of the loft which projects about 2ft (60 cm) east of the pew itself. The wooden wall of the loft on all three faces is decorated with two rows of rectangular panels filled with an elaborate fretted design of which the majority have been renewed, probably during Colonel Hamersley's ownership.

The loft was presumably used to accommodate musicians.

In the southern pew, the insides of all four partitions have been decorated with a design of stars with eight points within a garland, all gilded. Although shorter in the column the arcading above the west wall of this pew is similar to that in the northern pew, but it is broken into on the north side by the double doorway. A further series of short columns with Ionic capitals supports the domed canopy the vault of which, where not renewed, is painted with stars on a blue background. A well-carved rose, rather resembling a Tudor rose, is at the apex of the vaulting, The outside of the canopy is decorated with crocketed ribs which meet at the apex in a plain wooden base now housing one end of an iron stay attached to the wall but as late as 1883 it is said to have supported figures of the Virgin and Child. There may have been four other figures at the angles. Indeed one thought to represent Learning was still in existence in the 1920s. The canopy represents something of a throwback in style of about a century compared with the pew itself, but in actuality both are probably contemporary.

In the wall behind the panelling on the south side of the pew (and not now visible) is a trefoil-headed piscina with a round bowl just east of centre, and in this respect similar to the piscina in the sanctuary. This piscina shows that there was an altar against the southern half of the rood screen. Altars in front of the rood screen were fairly common - for example, at Patrishow in Powys and Ranworth in Norfolk, where there were altars on both the north and south sides of the screen. But at Rycote there is no trace of an altar on the north side, though there may well have been one.

It is generally held that the northern pew was erected about 1610, as the Norreys family pew, and that the southern one was set up especially for Charles I's visit in 1625. Though it cannot be definitely proved, the workmanship of the pews makes this a reasonable possibility. All that can be said with certainty is that both pews are early seventeenth century, though the canopy of the southern pew is of an older design.

There is a rise of one step into the chancel the floor of which has a diamond design in black and white. The fifteenth-century choir seating survives, including the return stalls against the rood screen. The seating is quite plain in design but terminates at the east on each side in a half poppy head. Above the seating on the north and south sides is an early seventeenth-century dado. The desk ends in a similar poppy head on each side against the central aisle and at the altar end. The front of the desk is decorated with blind trefoil-headed arcading.

The spiral altar rails are probably of the same date as the reredos. The altar table has four bulbous legs joined by a ledge near the base and with floral design in relief on the front and two sides but not at the back, showing that its position was always meant to be against the east wall. The wooden reredos is dated 1682 and the high standard of the work suggests an Oxford or London craftsman, though there is no evidence to attribute the work to Grinling Gibbons as has been done in the past. The much greater maturity of design and detail should be compared with the early seventeenth-century carving in the two pews, the pulpit and the earlier reredos.

The reredos is a fine example of English baroque church fittings. It follows the usual pattern of division into four. Its entablature breaks forwards over four fluted Corinthian columns and up into a segmental central pediment. Above is an attic (upper structure) with vases. The entablature and the panels are enriched. The tympanum of the pediment is filled with good-quality carving supported on slight brackets which break forward slightly in the entablature and are linked by a reverse curve section. This is below the central panel which is painted with the name of God in Hebrew, Greek, Latin and English, above which is a winged cherub's head. The columns frame enriched panels. The two in the centre (the Decalogue or Ten Commandments) are round headed and above are small segmental pediments; the flanking ones (the Pater or Our Father and Credo or Apostle's Creed) have small triangular pediments. Outer panels complete the composition; it is possible that they were painted with Moses and Aaron as the subjects.

When the reredos was removed during repair work, traces of a blocked doorway were found towards the northern end of the east wall. It is possible that this gave access to collegiate buildings sited to the east. In the south wall of the sanctuary is a wide trefoil-headed piscina with its circular bowl pierced with three drainage holes well to the east of centre, thus allowing part of the base to be used as a shelf.

Between the two windows in the south wall of the chancel is the only elaborate monument in the chapel. It is 'In Memory of the Right Honourable James Bertie Earl of Abingdon and Baron Norreys of Rycot, who died 22nd May AD 1699 *aetat* 46 and Elconora his wife eldest daughter and coheir of Sir Henry Lee of Ditchley . . . died 1691 *aetat* 33: The long inscription ends 'Willoughby the Present Earl in Obedience to the Will of his Great Uncle Montague Earl of Abingdon caused this monument to be erected AD MDCCLXVII.'

Above the inscription is a bust of the earl standing on a base surrounded by palm fronds, foliage, a book, a coronet and a sword, with a coat of arms on either side. At the base of the monument is a further coat of arms with eight quarterings supported on one side by a robed figure and on the other by an almost naked bearded man. It is a work of considerable merit but the sculptor is unknown.

On the opposite wall a plain tablet commemorates 'Montague Bertie Comitis de Abingdon necnon Baronis de Rycote' who died 16 October 1854.

On both lateral walls of the chancel are brackets which would formerly have held funeral helms and other achievements.

Two storeys of the tower were obviously fitted for domestic accommodation for a priest - rather surprisingly as there must have been collegiate accommodation nearby, although probably of a fairly modest nature. Here, too, the internal faces of the tower suggest that its top stage was modified at an early date, possibly during the actual course of building.

In the tower is the wooden Commandments board of 1610, which may have acted as or formed part of the reredos which preceded the present one. The Commandments, originally painted in gold but now faint, are contained within two compartments each surmounted by a flattened semicircular arch supported by plain circular columns with Ionic capitals. The spandrels of the arches are filled with carved foliage including an acorn and pomegranates and two birds, one of which has at some date been deliberately sawn off.

HISTORY

The descent of Rycote is clear from at least the fourteenth century when Nicolas Englefield, steward of Richard II's household, obtained the property by marriage. When he died in 1415 the estate passed by the marriage of Sibil, the elder of his two daughters, to Richard Quatremayne, a member of another Oxfordshire family. The 'brass' figures of Richard (died 1478) and Sibil (died 1483) (the latter now headless) lie on their table tomb in the south transept of Thame Church, 2½ miles east of Rycote.

Richard Quatremayne was a councillor to Richard, Duke of York, and to Edward IV. He endowed almshouses in Thame which were rebuilt by Lord Williams in the following century. Quatremayne built the present chapel, which was consecrated in 1449, and to it he attached a chantry foundation of three priests. Richard and Sibil died childless and the third and smaller 'brass' figure on their tomb probably represents Richard Fowler who was Sibil's nephew and Richard's godson, and it was to him that Rycote passed.

Richard Fowler, who was Chancellor of the Duchy of Lancaster from 1473 till his death in 1478, was succeeded by his son, another Richard, who was something of a spendthrift. In course of time he had to part with much of his landed property, including Rycote which he sold in 1521 to Sir John Heron who was treasurer of the household to Henry VII and Henry VIII. His son, Giles, sold the property to Sir John Williams, the first owner of Rycote who may be described as a figure of considerable national importance.

In all probability it was Williams who rebuilt the house in its quadrangular form,
if one may judge from the symmetrical design, stepped gables and cupola-crowned turrets shown in Winstanley's view. Williams worked in co-operation with his kinsman, Thomas Cromwell, and he was one of the visitors for Winchester, among other places, at the dissolution of the monasteries. As a result he became possessed of considerable monastic lands and he used a small part of his wealth for altruistic purposes; by his will he founded a grammar school at Thame where John Hampden was later to be a pupil. The original building still stands south of the church though now used as a private residence, the school having moved to a site on the Oxford road in 1879. Williams also rebuilt, in timber-framed style, the almshouses at Thame that had been founded by Richard Quatremayne.

Williams held various official positions under Henry VIII, Edward VI, Mary and Elizabeth. He helped to facilitate Mary's accession and it was during her reign that he became Baron Williams of Thame. As Sheriff for Oxfordshire he was in official attendance at the burning of the three Protestant Bishops, Cranmer, Latimer and Ridley, at Oxford. Mary appointed Williams one of the guardians of the Princess Elizabeth, and on occasions Elizabeth visited Rycote from the half retirement, half confinement of Woodstock Palace. Doubtless with an eye to the future, Williams treated the princess with much tact and kindness, and she preferred him to his fellow guardian, Sir Henry Bedingfield.

Lord Williams died on 14 October 1559 at Ludlow Castle where he was in residence in his capacity as President of the Council of the Marches of Wales. He and his wife, Elizabeth, lie in effigy on a stately table

12

tomb within its original grille in the middle of the chancel of Thame Church. This is not a unique position (there are other table tombs in a similar position at Cobham in Kent, Bottesford in Leicestershire, and Warwick), but what is unusual is that the figures face west and not east. There Lord Williams and his lady lie, he with beard neatly combed on top of his ruff. Round the sides of the tomb are the arms of their own family and those they were connected with by marriage (the Moores, the Wenmans, the Giffords, the Stavelys, etc), probably the work of the elder Gerard Johnson of the Southwark firm of sculptors.

Lord Williams was succeeded by his daughter Marjorie, who some time before 1545 had married Sir Henry Norreys. He was known to Elizabeth because he was living at Wytham, just northwest of Oxford and close to Woodstock Palace when Elizabeth was there under restraint during part of her sister's reign. He may have helped his father-in-law in his duties as the princess's custodian. Elizabeth may have felt a genuine sympathy for Norreys because his father, another Henry, had been executed as the alleged lover of Anne Boleyn. At any rate Elizabeth was fond of the Norreyses and after becoming Queen she stayed at Rycote several times. In 1566 she came in company with the Earl of Leicester, after visiting Oxford, and it was on this visit that Norreys was knighted. She came again in 1568 and 1570 and then not for 22 years. After six years as ambassador to France Sir Henry was created Baron Norreys of Rycote in 1572. In 1588 Leicester was here and addressed a letter to Elizabeth 'from your lodging at Rycott.' He died five days later and Elizabeth carefully marked the letter 'his last letter.'

In September 1592 Queen Elizabeth paid her last visit to Rycote, again coming from Oxford. In accordance with the custom of the times, Norreys greeted her arrival with a fulsome speech in which he declared 'I meane not to recount my service but to tell your Majesty that I am past al service, save devotion. My horse, mine armour, my shielde, my sworde, the riches of a young souldier, and an old souldier's reliques, I should here offer to your Highnesse; but my four boies have stalled them from me, vowing themselves to armes, and leaving me to my prayers. This is their resolution, and my desire, that their lives may be imployed wholy in your service, and their deathes be their vowes sacrifice. Their deathes, the rumour of which hath so often affrighted the Crowe my wife, that her hart hath bene as black as her feathers. I know not whether it be affection or fondness, but the Crowe thinketh her owne birds the fairest, because to her they are the dearest.'

On the following Sunday morning Elizabeth went into the garden where 'sweete musicke' was played and there she received four letters, one from Ireland, one from Flanders and two from Brittany, each accompanied by some valuable little gift. They were from the four Norreys sons serving abroad. The Norreyses had six sons in all. The eldest, William, had died on active service in Ireland in 1579. Four others were to die in similar circumstances before their father's death, three in Ireland and one in Brittany. With justification Camden described the Norreys boys as 'a brood of spirited, martial men.' When the second son, John, died in Ireland in 1597 Elizabeth sent a formal letter to Lady Norreys to which she added a postscript in her own hand. 'Myne owne Crowe, harme not thyselfe for booteles healpe; but shewe a good example, to comfort your dolorous yokefellow.'

Lord Norreys died in 1601 and was buried at Rycote, like many of the Norreyses and their successors, the Berties, till about 1886. Ford and Lady Norreys (who had died in 1599) are commemorated by a sumptuous monument in the east aisle of the north transept of Westminster Abbey, a product of the Southwark workshops and probably by Isaac James, a partner of the better-known sculptor Nicholas Stone. Lord and Lady Norreys lie on a marble sarcophagus around which kneel their six sons. Eight Corinthian columns support a flat canopy above which is a centrepiece the north and south sides of which depict military scenes, doubtless showing their sons' martial exploits. Above all is a figure of Mercury.

Lord Norreys was succeeded by his one surviving son, Sir Edward, who himself died in 1603, when Rycote passed to his nephew, Francis, who held the title Earl of Berkshire, and was the son of Edward's eldest brother William. Francis committed suicide at Rycote in 1622 by shooting himself, so it was said, with a crossbow. He had apparently become unbalanced in his mind, the result of a term in the Fleet Prison for assaulting Lord Scrope in a passage in the House of Lords when the House was sitting with the King in attendance. His daughter, Elizabeth, succeeded him.

Elizabeth was the wife of Edward Wray, Groom of the Bedchamber to James I, and it was during their ownership that Charles I came to stay at Rycote in 1625, a year of plague in London when Court and Parliament moved to Oxford. Their daughter Bridget married (as her second husband) Montagu Bertie, second Earl of Lindsey. Their elder son was James, created Earl of Abingdon in 1682. He died in 1699 and was buried at Rycote. During his lifetime and that of his son, Rycote became the meeting place of the local High Church and Jacobite faction.

In October 1745, the house was partly destroyed by a fire in which died the heir, another James Bertie (great-grandson of his namesake), aged ten. The house was never rebuilt on its original scale but what survived was made into the present house by William Weir for Lieutenant-Colonel A St G Hamersley, who had bought what had degenerated into farm property. In 1952 the chapel was placed in the guardian-ship of the Ministry of Works by the then owner, Mr M G A C Michaelis. In 1984 it transferred to the care of English Heritage.

Since 2000, the new owners, Mr and Mrs Taylor, have restored the house, including what remained of the original house after the fire. Mr Taylor has set up a charitable trust for the maintenance of the chapel.

Detail of canopied pew : boss at apex of vault

GLOSSARY

Achievement   In heraldry, a complete display of armorial bearings

Arcade   Series of arches supported on columns or piers; *blind arcade*, the same applied to a surface

Baluster   Short pillar supporting a handrail

Buttress   Vertical projection from a wall to give additional strength or to resist the lateral thrust of an arch or roof

Capital   Uppermost feature of a column or shaft, often decorated

Cartouche   Ornamental panel in the form of a scroll, usually bearing an inscription and sometimes ornately framed

Chancel   Eastern part of a church reserved for clergy and choir, generally divided from the nave by a screen or railing (*cancellus*), from which the name is derived

Chantry   An endowment for the maintenance of priests to sing masses for the departed soul of the donor; also a body of priests so endowed

Cinquefoil   Five-lobed plan

Corinthian   One of the three Grecian orders of architecture, having bell-shaped capitals with rows of acanthus leaves and usually fluted columns

Crocket   Small ornamental design usually in the form of a bud or curled leaf

Cupola   Small dome crowning a roof

Dripstone   Projection normally over a door or window to deflect rainwater

Entablature   Horizontal member above a classic column, often used without the column

Finial   Ornament at the top of a spire, gable, arch, etc

Ionic   One of the three Grecian orders of architecture characterised by capitals decorated with spiral scrolls (volutes)

Light   Part of a glazed window or opening for light

Mullion   Upright dividing a window or other opening into two or more lights; *transom* is the horizontal member

Pediment   Low-pitched gable-end form with a decorative rather than functional use in Classical and Renaissance architecture above a portico, doors, windows, niches, etc

Piscina   Carved shallow basin with a drain in a wall niche near the altar, for washing sacred vessels

Quatrefoil   Four-lobed plan

Reredos   Ornamental screen at the back of an altar

Rood loft   Gallery above a *rood screen*

Rood screen   Division between the nave and the quire of a church, surmounted by a crucifix

Spandrel   Triangular area above the haunch of an arch; space between the shoulder of an arch and a surrounding square frame

Strapwork   Decoration consisting of interlaced bands

String course   Moulding or projecting band running horizontally across the façade of a building or around the walls

Tracery   Intersecting ribwork in the upper part of a window

Trefoil   Three-lobed plan

Vault   Arched roof or ceiling usually in stone, sometimes supported or articulated by stone ribs